# John Harbison

# MIRABAI SONGS

## for Soprano (or Mezzo-Soprano) and Piano

### English versions by Robert Bly

### AMP-7977

ISBN 978-0-7935-5913-8

## Associated Music Publishers, Inc.

DISTRIBUTED BY

HAL•LEONARD®
CORPORATION
7777 W. BLUEMOUND RD. P.O. BOX 13819 MILWAUKEE, WI 53213

Mirabai's ecstatic religious poetry was written in 16th-century India. When she was 27, her husband was killed in a war. Mirabai refused to die on her husband's funeral pyre, as was the custom. Instead, she left her family compound, wrote her poems to Krishna, the Dark One, and sang and danced them in the streets.

1. It's True, I Went to the Market
2. All I was Doing was Breathing
3. Why Mira Can't Go Back to Her Old House
4. Where Did You Go?
5. The Clouds
6. Don't Go, Don't Go

This work was first performed on September 9, 1983, Susan Larson, soprano, Craig Smith, piano. Performance time: 17 minutes.

The work is also available in a version for voice and chamber ensemble, for which the present version can serve as a vocal score. The chamber version has been recorded by Northeastern Records, under the composer's direction, and by Nonesuch Records, with David Zinman conducting. Materials for the ensemble version, which is scored for alto flute, bass clarinet, percussion, harp, violin, viola, cello and bass, are available from the G. Schirmer Rental Department.

# MIRABAI SONGS

for Soprano (or Mezzo-Soprano) Voice and Piano

English versions
Robert Bly

John Harbison
(1982)

*To Janice Felty*
## 1. It's True, I Went to the Market

N.B. Pedal marks are indicated only if their duration is not intuitively clear.

**Tempo I** ( ♩ =108)

Be with me when I lie down; _ Be with me, be with me when I lie down; _____

ritardando

**Meno mosso** ( ♩ =96)

You prom - ised me this _____ in an

ear - li - er life. _____

(non cresc.)

*To Jan DeGaetani*

# 2. All I Was Doing Was Breathing

shoul - ders          what - ev - er you want    to       say     of    me.

Mi - ra says:___

With - out the   en - er - gy____ that lifts      moun - tains,___

how   am    I    to      live?____

poco arpeggiando

*To Susan Larson*

# 3. Why Mira Can't Go Back to Her Old House

*To D'Anna Fortunato*

# 4. Where Did You Go?

movendo poco a poco

and then walked in-land, leav - ing the boat in — an

o - - - - - - cean of part - - - ing.—

Tempo I (♩=66)

Mi - ra says: Tell me when you will come to

meet me.—

*To Joan Heller*

# 5. The Clouds

**Andante velato** ( ♩ = 88 )

*p*

*p*

When I saw the dark clouds, I wept, O Dark____

One, I wept at the dark clouds.

*poco cresc.*

Black clouds___ soared___ up, and took some yel - low a -

*mp*

*p, subito*

The one I love lives past those fields; ____ rain has fal - len on my

bod - y, ____ on my hair, ____ as I wait, as ___ I wait ____

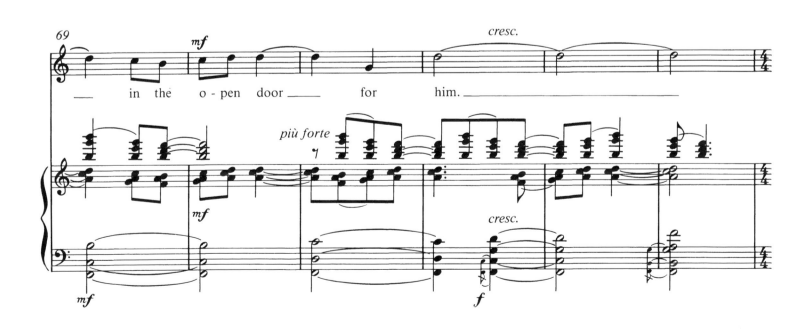

____ in the o - pen door ____ for him. _____

*To Susan Quittmeyer*

# 6. Don't Go, Don't Go

Token Creek Wisc., September 1982